Parade
of
Malfeasance

(some)other books by EMP

Bury My Heart In The Gutter
by Dan Denton

my lungs are a dive bar
by Walter Moore

Those Who Favor Fire, Those Who Pray To Fire
by Ben Brindise & Justin Karcher

Trail Her Trash
by Lola Nation

#Beer
by Ezhno Martín

Ten-Foot-Tall and Bulletproof
by Jason Ryberg

Feeding The Monster
by Michael Grover and Adrian Lime

Little Jenny Sue
by Jeanette Powers

Route 23 to Golgotha
by J. Ian Bush

Parade Of
Malfeasance

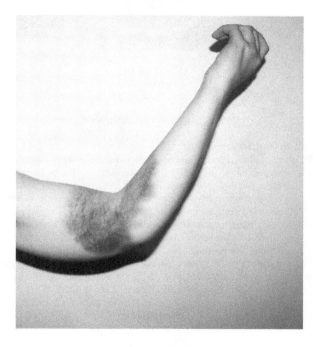

Poems
Joseph Goosey

Columbus, Ohio
empbooks.com

First Edition:
ISBN: 978-0-9997138-6-0
LOC: 2020933531
10 19 33 34 6 11 1973

Design, Layout, and Edits: Ezhno Martín
Photos: The Anti-Social Section of the Internet (Aisle 5)

TOC

Leaving Las Vegas II

Say that a life's in thirds
then consider cruelty
as if fundamental.

Alicia Silverstone gets cast
as your ambassador
to the less privileged.

It's a decision
that doesn't play well
inside the diaphragm
of your public:

a fickle eagle with a hole
thirsty for grandstands
            backslash
the lowercase flag
tepid from papa's laments
            backslash
debtor's jailbait.

This year's prize
goes to those bold enough
to not yet murder us in our sleep.

The aforementioned is evidence
of brains gone poisoned.

So thin's the condom
between whatever this is right now
and the ingenuity

convincing the wielders of lasers
to hold off a little longer
from eradicating

this sweet sweet populace.

Chapter I

...gone from us,
it would be like taking a piece of all of us
and throwing it away — Ted Bundy's mom

The time I was roofied
by an older horse trainer
while chugging malbec, he told me
the blue inside my reddened eyes
was *getting* [him] *so hard.*

Nobody else
was willing to touch me or
I was afraid

(the names of all the others
dissolve in tannins)

which is to say
that had he bothered to ask
I would've allowed him
to get all up in this
or at least
I would've allowed him
to swallow these future scientists.

Instead, he didn't ask
so I fell asleep
at the wheel
as is customary.
I hit a pine
got woke
by being poked
by a cop

who I would've sucked wholly,
pre-dash cam style,

in exchange
for a blanket.

So there's that
and the extinction
of tree kangaroos,
not nearly as predictable

as the cruelties
of our imagination

when we wish to get wet.

State Of The Union

If my wife can't bed the entire Midwest,
who owns the rights?

Jeff Bezos could send each American
$433 plus or minus
the fair market price of my habits.

Last year I tried to get a job
in the customer service department at *kink.com*

and got flogged
with the audible silence of lacking.

I wanted to be certain the citizenry
was being tied up
beyond satisfaction.

Mischa Barton,
did she collapse
or am I thinking of us?

Ghosts Won't Keep The Baby Product Royalties Rolling

Skewwhiff goes the muppetry
by which *Welcome* is meant
& Marie Antoinette
The Remix is in the building
pissing hot upon the diggers
from first class feat. husband
who's got nothing but the finest
of predatory feed sticks
impaling all available cavities &
the outside of this building
has that *heads of other humans*
are inside of this building vibe
or aura or whatever it is while
whatever this happens to be
needn't ever actually be
while fiscal responsibility
is bile for the gen-pop &
blood floods the admin
while playing hostage sitch
inside of Fort Knox all like
Looky Daddy, The Money
it's a thin ass piece with two Cs
claiming conspiracy
while railing lines of flour
from a poverty tit
while *X's* cover any offense
By which *Sorry* isn't meant
& Marie squats on our noseface
'cause there's a blindfold

which we forgot &
also the great pleasure gerbil
of '92 — long decayed —
doing his dang shimmy
inside the classified &
checkered dance floor carcass
of the department
of ethics & accountability
so ensues a tire fire
& none of the afterlife

The Nineties Were Wild

Regime change is the new grunge.
Regime change is also the old world grunge.

John Bolton's not immortal.
This isn't *John Bolton: Mythologies.*

That was Sub Zero
just like the Illinois of today
and your welcome back reception
filled with non-alcoholic refreshments,
rice pilaf and dejection.

Feeling abrasive tonight?
Petulance got you dry?
Try abjection in the form of nostalgia.

Anyone who's read Noam's Failed States
knows the damn drill.

The drill:
she's damned,
so eat your loaf.

Whatever your dad did for oil
won't be remembered by Puck or Judd.

Instead of shooting the television,
we snort fat lines off it. Socialism
bleeds out in the tall ass grass.
I throw the cardigan from my back
and into the trash.

Inside Caracas,
it's 73 and sunny.

As Supposedly Wise Men Assess The Damage

As agriculture collapses
I've got my plate of eggs
and porn for days.

Like

have you ever seen
such a habitat in binaries?

The tree kangaroo has.

We're going extinct, right?
So now's a time to tell the sister
she never appeared in mirrors.

EBT won't intervene.

In The Citadel tonight
we scrimp on our safe words.

If Spiders Weighed 238lbs

Servals have the fastest paw strike
of any living feline.
Blue whales have the biggest babies
and if spiders weighed 238lbs
maybe then we'd give a fuck
while hailing our methods humane

but for now our capillaries
chug Keystone,
pixelated worlds become womb,
cassowaries won't eat a local newborn,
and swapping out urinal cakes
pays nine an hour
plus transportation

to and from
whatever holes we crawl.

This ecology is too spicy.
Remember the declaration of independence
from ever again cooking with jalapeño
before buttstuffs?

Once
there was a tiger who choked
on a good time.

Once
there was a boy who ached granular.

Once
those two bred
and a children's book was sold...

...the author of which is a scumbag.

We sing a hymn in her honor.

Aside From Wild Fires Not Being
License Plates And Even If

1

Contested results
of the late disgraced *sorting hat*©
leave us constant,
sleepless. Economy

of language isn't what we're about.
A coalition of the unwilling is

however lost
deep fried in the thorax. Feeling glum?
Check out our appetizers, so sure
not to amaze.

2

With the QA Department
cirrhosis pends

while the comments section
at *The Intercept*

never pairs well
with the depression
you call chips n' cheese.

3

One season

hell adjacent
in the capital

Our nest egg
got embayed

by employees
of *Live Jasmin*

/

Regrets
are this WiFi
horse-like
in the womb.

4

After stealing all the plants and mail

I became paranoid
about surveillance
with hardly a thought
to the oppression of periods

UPS sent a reply
stating my application

had not met minimum
requirements

Meanwhile
in the Markov Process

a keg stand

Annual Assessment

Such hostility toward our leisure tonight!

Blaise Cendrars, for instance,
is a speed-zombie
making his bed
in our litter boxes
while my wife might leave me
for the proprietor
of an inn on cold nights.

You know those nights
with beer in mugs fit for D&D,
fit for that one campaign
you promise your friends
someday you'll get together
to finish
but know —

the next human
to request a fax
will be subject
to a grand unspooling.

Having squandered the gifts
granted by her in whom
I refuse to believe
like a Quincy Jones quip, I notice
Selena Gomez is trying to kill us
by wearing that sweatshirt, knowing
a photo will fetch $175
in the year of somebody's lord

it's raining down at the mine brothel.

My herringbone-twenties
were an avoidable deficit.
Holler if you feel the heat

of your grandpa's vodka

anchoring this sallow.

I've yet to cross a single border
and throughout I've lived
during wartime. Separate
from the tigers synonymous
with Siberia. On the Amtrak
I was asked if I'd ever been
to Burning Man. *I have anxiety*
is my answer to all inquiries.
While envisioning veridical
in that sleeper car I pushed
cirrhosis through to QA
only to have cirrhosis
returned for revision
but the quality of breakfast
is near mint condish.

The sphere of influence
may not water down the regime
but will decrease my credit score

in record breaking ways.
I want to tell you about my travels,
thing is — they'll never occur.
Constantly celebrity

assaults our mutual field of vision.
Corporate tie-ins to the birth of your daughter

will not haunt in the form
I'd hope they'd haunt.

Money is all about the access

screams Jacob Marley,
snorting lines and ranting
about increased interest rates. Foreigners
have cursed our babies.

Get that detergent cash
for you deserve it. An essay
on entitlements
is how we began courtship.
Look at us now.

Fresh off the Zoodler,
nauseously tanned,
needing for naught
wanting for all. After all

the schedule is checked.
The train to promised acres
has been canceled on account

of being too spooky.
From ingesting our lineage

to fortifying future kidney stones,
what a long, unnecessary trip
it hasn't been.

For your emotional support squirrel
the congregation is grateful.

Bio-power is a cruel myth
for the comfortably sad.

Being among the faithful
is one element of sustenance.

The only the other,
studies conclude,
is brutal.

So we arrive
at an exit tonight,

achingly lit.
Stage right, always

stage left.

Dead Kids Make Profitable TV

When a president speaks
I catch his mint stench. I think
everyone is a poet
presenting problems
in my machete identity.

Where to go? *The water,*
she's off the civet screams
I think teal is my spirit hummer.

The novelty shop caught fire
in a specific format,
unequal to desire.

When you price those cages
my tissue unfurls. It's so inappropes
to think of the crematorium
as you refresh the spit
preventing a blow.

SOMETHING ONGOING

Best call Lambda.

The tit milk has spilt
and despite a couple of decent dinners
I completely forget his name. I think
it was George but what seems important
hardly ever is.

After sucking a poem or two
out of him in May
I quit saying there was time for another glass of wine.

I quit saying there was time for anything
because I was working on this long poem
or at least saying
that's what was happening
at night. I had begun seeing cats
running across the floor
before living with any cats and also
neglecting to pay the rent
and you care
little about this
but I'm trying
to be open as possible
which often includes
saying shit nobody wants to hear
so what I mean
by saying I sucked a poem or two
out of him in May is that he learned
that by two or three in the afternoon
I'd be amenable to just about anything,
especially if it involved
free Scaloppini.

In the mornings after I'd come to,
for only a couple of hours,
just to make a record of our transactions and transgressions.

Occasionally my father stepped in
to act competent on my behalf.

Occasionally something echoes bye.

You might say *Christ*
but simply going to brunch sometimes is all three nails.

Grassroots campaigns are
self-sucking cows
and I knew a woman once,
still do,
who listed the fact
that I failed to purchase a specific item
from the Tiffany's catalogue
as a firm reason to bade us farewell as fuck all.
She's now a recruiting manager
for the Peace Corps
at the U. of Vermont and
sometimes during sleep
people change.

Having driven past
all the former apartments
and having burnt all of the alms

sometimes
we regress as a team.
I want nothing to do with these 40 lashes. My fears
get tossed out with the recycling.

I become paranoid in the act. The third,
to be specific. Goodnight.

There's snow

let's drown. A country
is in my thighs tonight
and a cat raises complaints
while returning a Kenneth Cole suit.

Noam Chomsky once got the better of me
in a DC Peruvian bar
dollar tequila shot for dollar tequila shot
because Noam simply had more dollars.

He was great. Certainly,
I agreed with everything
he had to say. I think
it may've been the dollar tequila, tho.
Everyone has their tricks.

I pass out on the pavement.

I could use a referee for daily activities.

Whether or not I agreed with their calls,
suggestions for alternative action could be made.

This information could be synthesized
sanctified or
burnt up in a tire fire
on the Halloween of your choosing.

Today we remember those
who died by choice
as Bruce Springsteen sprays a load
while straddling a giant eagle.

New Jersey is where it's at when you own a white rabbit and
have the proper backing.
In tents we shared our best of nights.

I speak in plurals now. Between the cats,
yous, and you, little track can be kept

save for the dots on our arms.

Did I mention the baby? Yeah,
I'm involving a baby
simply to take us there
as a test of solidarity. All I ask of this life
is a scrabble partner who will cheat with abandon.

Sporting sweat and gangrene
just exiting the ninth best night of her life

the pants have been cast off into the ether
and there is a lack of massacre on Broad street.

If only I could open my eyes
early enough to document the failure.

A heart beats exclusive from its extensions.

As a family we do not look forward to progress.

A town hall style meeting was held
and we ran away
with our individual slices of rum cake and regret.

There is a common bond
between the storage closet, contacts, and trash.

Buffalo Wild Wings did dictate our Tuesdays
while in the animal hospital: a decree

put me down for stamped and screaming.

I want to know
what would be cause
for involuntary emancipation
by which I mean

strap me down in the basement of Belk

set fire to that shit

and move to Truth Or Consequences.

Snitching has never been my New England of choice.

When clams gather they tend to unionize
and my visions are not yet prepared for such allergies.

For some reason
now we're on yacht.
Nobody knows
how to keep it from capsizing.

The nautical whatever is assumed in this mortal game of
Scrabble.

Somewhere
ensconced in nylon
somebody cries
a North American cry

elsewhere
rugs are spun by the month
and given away in exchange for green beans and gallons
of beers you'll never drink.

Say Uh OH
and get wild in the river.

By the way
we're drinking orange juice by the full moon.
Keep that shit on deny.

numbers numbers numbers numbers…
…way too far gone
to be doing maths.

The insane portion of my ribs says *No Thanks*
but the O'Hara of my ribs screams *YAY*

Nobody does it all night.
I don't give a solitary shit about the project
from which you hail.
Nobody does it all night.

Your English class was a toilet
and sometimes the metro is crowded as that one
rally for sanity
that turned otherwise.

Crictor knew best the way to freedom:
Please others
and their view of you turns sunny.

What is required,
what is preferred,
and what is essential
is all off
buying crack in the slums
of our wooden rollercoaster dream.

If I die today
it would be less noted
than the merger of major energy providers

and while we're on the subject
of prostitutes:
who isn't?

Most people
are looking for a partner,
someone to get poor with,
someone they can hope dies
way after they do.

Most people are looking for a sense of permanence
and instead most people are taking a course
on managerial statistics,
getting free coffee and croissants,
chicken breasts
and rice pilaf.

Where I'm going with all this
was supposed to be the center.

My cat aches and the river's attune.

I don't know what it says
about the state of North Carolina
that the liquor store opens at eight
and closes at eight.

I don't know what it says
about my current state,
that Geoff at the counter
already has my order rang up
before I pass the off duty cop.

I don't know what it says,
mommy,
can you read it for me?

Crictor knew best
how to squelch the side affects.

Transgressions and transactions
have been recorded every morning
in which I manage to come to
for a couple of hours.
Free Scaloppini
gets regurgitated
into or around the toilet
and I am now amenable to just about anything.
It is after three in the afternoon
and after May (as it is always
after May) I spit a poem or two
back into his navel and onto his lint.
I'm trying to be
open as possible
which is always difficult
with to whom you say love. You should know
the back rent's paid,
that my cat curls in the corner.
With a nail I've carved this all
into the wall. There is still no time
for anything but more wine. I think
now his name is Leonard,

which was never really important

and despite a couple of decent dinners
I no longer care.

It'd really be for the best
if someone would just call Lambda.

Our water:

she's broken.

To The Harbor, To The Wayside, Let All This Mice Plague Crawl

When I was young,
32 years ago, I wanted to be
a poet with a crap life. This year
I just want a couch with springs
that won't jam into our asses
in ways we don't desire. It's a hot verve
filled with residency requirements,
funeral rites, registration fees,
and out of body experiences
so intense we forget our license
must be renewed
in order to continue
making the kind of living
not suitable for children.

The Tragic Life of

Please pummel me hotly into the digestion suite,
I asked of my wife as she lapped at the integration.

Drowning impetuously in volleyball thighs,
I bequeath my admin passcode to the whorl.

As my stye hurdles toward reckoning,
IRS employees receive a paycheck

and the JP Morgan squirrel
goes unexplained.

Finances got you limp?
Try avoiding your friends.

Absolution got you in debt?
Try imagining a world without tigers.

My proximity to putting servals to sleep
stokes fears with a real turd for the books. Sometimes

at my job I stare into the faces of celebrities
who will never lick my abscess. Did you know?

How dark it is inside this place
is right up there with the greats. Forever young

among the tourists traps we heave,
in constant search of parking.

Attack Of The Clones

but my goal's not to stop smokin'
and not to stop drinkin',
it is to become the kindest floozy
in the most compassionate whorehouse.

At 18 I was handed a diploma
which demanded I *dream big*
and enter wherever
I feel welcome
in oncoming traffic.

Having sang too much
about holes
and too little
about optimism

it's too late for us. Now
circling the yard
in my pickup
like an uncle
who steals from his employer.

Meanwhile
throughout 2010
I was obsessed
with an inside-the-beltway
financial dominatrix
whose sessions I couldn't afford
so instead I went wonky
in thrift store fashions. Later
on *Live Jasmin*

I converted tips to tokens,
searched for a friend,
found evidence
of collusion, requested
humiliation
of the affected variety.
I hurt my partner

by wanting to be hurt
by others.

Honest now, I hear
harnesses are hot,
in vogue. Let's be
contemporary

with one another.

Some Utopia

My wife's getting ready for work.

We're told
we're a lucky pair of bastards.

We're told we're privileged
to be paying three bucks
to see how little
there really is.

In the kitchen
we pretend to be grebes:

heads up,
proud of mistakes,
not breeding,
exhibiting
the core values
of a foundation.

The Koch brothers refuse
to go down on us.

Some utopia this exodus turned out to be.

Even Peter Thiel won't pay
with imaginary tokens
while visiting my cam4 channel.

Moaning
Wut Toys U Got
he is not.

I Spit On Your Grave (2010) Was A Waste Of 108 Minutes And So Is This

The world's oldest woman
might not have been. Her daughter
might have been instead.

To avoid inheritance taxes,
so says the research
conducted by a god complex.

From the bathroom, a song
recommends *go fuck* [my]*self*
and I might but not before

I snort these tariffs for compliance
purposes. A porpoise
enters consciousness, says

Screw this. We're out.

EVOQ

I'm not entirely sure who's where anymore (and/or of your birthday). Seems to me that the selection is all in the bone — form and function, she says (the one who is the baby in her belly; the one who won't break the news) — the cornerstone of every decent relationship. The cornerstone of every decent relationship is how one reacts to your sin (and/or whether or not one actually believes there is something that can be called a sin). Fashionable is your hat — and fashionable is my lack thereof. What spots are these. What spots are the reason you're now ignored. You couldn't get it up. It is all in the sex. The opposite is a lie that is told by loved ones and the truth is only told in rap songs. All the ascetical lambs in the tri-state area won't soothe your wounds (the wounds become *wounder*). Are we in or are we out of quotes? I can't remember whether or not the Slovenian was a fan of the Backstreet Boys. I can't remember what I ate but woke up pregnant (cheese — in all likelihood it was cheese; when in doubt, *cheese.*) Concentrate on the bones — you couldn't get it up. You say you a rude boy but you couldn't get it up (because you are nervous — will always be nervous, will always be secondary). I hesitate to say always, but *always.* A knife is in the sink. Now a cup. A knife and a cup. Such a cute couple. What else could we need (you couldn't get it up). You say you a rude boy but you couldn't get it up. You were so afraid to trifle.

Choking And Somewhat Serious About It

I've three-fourths of a mind
to crash this four-wheeler
into the abandoned greenhouse

might discover what the detectives have failed to
might hide it from them
might get charged with conspiracy
so derivative is the nonsense and thought

I came here to explain what aches
and what does ache
is that you're a goddamned lighthouse

golden showering the only road out of town
the frequency of unhealthy behavior
is being dialed up by the gnome we'd fired weeks ago

There is a discrepancy
between the need to be alone
and the pheromones each night

wasted on the rug

I am not
seeking anyone
maintaining a stable relationship with Christ
but if you've got one
I wouldn't mind meeting y'all at Chili's during
Two — 4 — One

I've qualms

      my comments card
      has gone unanswered

District Of Columbia Fetish Circa '10

they wanted more ketchup they were in town for a spanking
the best view available was that of the woman reading of hills
a corresponding dance was done and a third wall was broken
they came to order steak what they received was cheap latex

reading of hills she
reading of hills she

asked to be left alone

while we slapped one another with cedar the latex wasn't
leather
and our vessels were so inauthentic we did dance tho we
danced
until asked to please leave there was a glitter and there was
vodka
and there was a flogging a cage
a Saran human burrito we

said hello to our townhouse
were embarrassed

considered the word *tourist*

BABYSITTING

1:40PM
    in our demilitarized portion of living
                    across of course
    from a golf course
            the wolves revolve
       what insipid shit
    gets contrived in the outliers

The International Monetary Fund
                won't quit playing games with my
                    heart

Maggot Therapy
      a decent title
for something but
    where to put
        it

      I'm hardly a grass fed species
        and once
    distraught
I tossed the salad of a friend

          who cared no more
          for the way in which I'd hurt him
       than he did for the art
in which I'd no choice
    but to participate

          Fucking strange

    happenings
sitting here at the table

of a soon to be brother-in-law
making certain his six y/o daughter
doesn't die

for at least four hours
                    as we occupy ourselves
                    in our own silly ways

Responsibility

                              Fucking Strange

            on this table is a math problem
                  the homework of a fifteen y/o
who has just had a shoplifting case

                    dropped

in North Carolina Juvenile Court

congrats to her

                  I've never understood maths
                never intend to understand
how to go on in such daylight

y=a(x-int1)(x-int2)
y=a

                    is to me
                    a shitty piece
                    of conceptual writing

Jenny says it's all in the process
                        then we agree

It's all in the

head

we're each in a process
of becoming   The six y/o
is doing a headstand
has been   for hours

talking to herself
about beverages

There but for
she keeps on saying

Last night
on the phone with my mom
I listed the ways
in which the Catholic church
evicted the child

right out of a self
who was frightened
of asteroids

mainly
their immediacy

π π π

y=a(x-7)(x-1)

Why
does *Y*
always got to equal *A*

it's not my responsibility to respond

Flushing may occur
just as anything
            may occur

A life so heavy

            is not recommended for tissue so delicate
                        but here I sit
                  beside a novel
                  Don't Try To Find Me
it's called and appears
                  to be about a daughter and mother
who keep secrets from each other and
                  more devastatingly
                              says the book jacket
      from themselves

I am tired
      of so much devastation

y=10/9(x-7)(x-1)

                        whatever that means
            at least *Y* doesn't equal *A* this time
                        unless *A*
                  is the solution
                  I'll never know

$$\pi \ \pi \ \pi$$

                  A crumpled up note on the table
which I've now made not crumpled
            because the preview was appealing

            reads *Sophocles says:*

Don't sleep with your mom

It's either a poem
        or notes for some honors class
whatever Sophocles said
                I've never known

Cattulus maybe

        another mistake entirely
                   I remember
                when what filled my days was qualified
                      by some form of merit

Like

        you are this or that

because you did

        or you didn't

Goddamn

now I just sit in front of a screen
for eight or nine hours a day
simply to be told
        things are important
when things are not important
for $13.26 an hour   I pretend to care
All forms of work are a form
            of pretending

Labor
skilled or unskilled
paid or unpaid
     like right now

           unskilled
        and unpaid

π π π

Grapefruit

is listed in all caps   (GRAPEFUIT)
as a contraindication
of this medicine   (for the cock)
which I've stolen
       off my friend's kitchen counter

I figure any drugs
          left on a kitchen counter
    are fair game
and that he'd understand
the nature of this experiment

which might be
what makes us friends

       an acceleration begins to manifest
         by which I mean
       watch out
for moving trains in this kind of century

Ellen'll be here soon

For her I'm grateful

       Not to spurt holy
         all over your chest
       all over your burning bush
         I'm feeling a little saved

For all the hospitals in which I've stayed

> *One look out a widow*
> *would make a difference.*

is a sentence
thought of

while looking out a window

It could be the rain
but windows allow me to imagine
I'm in London
                Maybe
I'm still in the hospital
                but shit
at least I'm in London and o my
                        how I've experienced
a decrease in motor skills
                Exclamations
are rare
I like them
as one does a lamb burger

                        questionably microbial

I open to the first page
of a book containing the blurb
                Chillingly plausible

I laugh
inside and read a line
                I'd kill

for a
    what
in response

π π π

It's been concluded Ellen will not be here soon or ever again
inside her head she's adopted the schedule of Anna Wintour

The fashion world is not OZ

The fashion world is the shakes
and cleaning the toilet with the shakes

π π π

I remain grateful but unholy
as whatever you think unholy

Tonight a friend asked me if I knew
        any good reads about Sophocles

I've another friend in high school
                who's been banned from Belk
she'll sum up Sophocles
                with a ukulele performance

        I think all of this and I say none

Tonight there is cause for retreat

π π π

About the job market
yet another friend said

                        The outlook is bleak

        I agree
                on all fronts

π π π

Next month I'll be in Florida for a holy union
and to tell my psychiatrist the ideation sits around
as though it's a bill I don't intend to pay
until threatened

                with disconnection of service

π π π

If this is to be about family
then it must also   by default
be about aching

        I say to the six y/o
when she selects for me which character I'll be
while playing twenty twenty-five-minute rounds
of Super Smash Brothers

She laughs as if she understood
            all that about aching

π π π

With a couple of stuffed animals we make noises
I say *yip yip spit spit yoshi yoshi woop woop*

        What I say in this context
       Doesn't matter for shit

                woop woop

π π π

I aim to become more proletariat by the day

I miss

I mean no living becomes earned
Just waking up should accompany a stipend

π π π

Leaving for wine now
Leaving this open
for other creatures to scrawl their opinions

π π π

Forgotten dolls make way for forgotten everything otherwise

π π π

If Bowser isn't the oldest
but has a bunch of children
who are you to say the children are not older

How do you know

now theorizing
with a six y/o

woop woop

π π π

I've taken to reading the supposed classics
littering

your childhood bedroom
which is also your current bedroom
                              with bottles

π π π

Woke at 2:13AM
              frightened
of where the bay had gone

π π π

          I wonder
whether I successfully hang myself
with the entirety of this curling ribbon
              Don't worry
          not that you would worry
but don't worry
It's simply a question
of logistics   a question
of practicality   a question
of ridding oneself   a question
of redundancies

Too much asparagus
Too little piss

Too languid a lifestyle
Too petty a theft

I'm no associate
or adjunct
or operator
I can   however
crash four wheelers
into such winding of vines

π π π

In the parking lot of the   LEGOLAND HOTEL
I assembled the   LEGO helicopter
      It didn't fly as far as we'd planned
         you slept the whole way back
we didn't fly   as far as I'd planned

π π π

I've been a terrible friend
     not meeting the new edition to the fam

     being in your new house
now makes me feel myself
         such an amputee

π π π

I haven't cum in a couple of weeks
     don't want to accidentally have a baby with a flea

        documentation from *FASTMED*
    states I've postpartum depression

π π π

Remember
     we used to buy food
     we used to buy food
you'd nap
while I cooked the food

for one
I bought the Valentine's special for two

the cats did the napping

I was out of Morton's

so tears it was

π π π

There won't ever be anyone to talk to
　　　　about individualized decline

π π π

No bog is too
　　　　　but O yeah they so are
Once
　　　　confused and cut
by what I claimed was a dog
　　　　everyone knew
was imaginary
　　　　I received

THE LOWEST GRADE IN THE CLASS

　　　　　　I attempted to argue
　　　　that grades and what both I
　　　　　　　　as student
　　　　　and Erik
　　　　　　　　as teacher
were attempting to do mattered
　　　　　　　　none at all
on the scale of global materialism
　　　　suffering harvesting you choose
　　　　　　　a verb or noun and shove it inside the
throat

I offered to discuss
this crisis   of faith

        he called it
over a drink
                a beer I said
but Erik
        who'd not simply given such a low grade
                but had made a point
                        to declare he'd done so
                as fact *as if by*
        commandment
        declined
only coffee for me these days
                he said
and maybe
        that was the reason
he felt compelled to inform another person
        how shitty they were doing
                in comparison to their peers
despite operating
        inside totally inconsequential bubble
and maybe
                it was a reason
        I decided to exit
                        My bones

screaming

                        you people

You're not as fun as I'd thought

L DOES NOT EQUAL A. NOT HERE. NOT EVER.

Somebody's endangered the porcupette!

I woke
sweating and stable. I haven't told my family
I've been weaning the mush off chemicals. Soon
I'll be afraid I'm not telling you too. Soon
you're to be family. On what date do we melt?
Soon I'll be so fucking afraid that the inverse-now
becomes a shared reality. To abandon you
in the stuff of nightmares that is a local SEARS
would be punishable by experiencing utopia.

Greed For Sensation
Will Not Be Permitted
As Documentary Evidence

The walls felt a rasp
for the entirety of an anchorless summer
Probably the one
during 2016
It was an asinine period
scheduled to be discounted
by the history
of recorded religions
and jackasses
I sat in this chair
a gift from human resources
because probably [I] *like drugs*
I was hanging out
inside a second life
since I couldn't manage
to get poked
by spending time
inside of the first
Similar to the first
the second life
was near empty with totality
and I'd dress the body
of the avatar
the way you dressed your Bitmoji
tonight
with accuracy and care
but also
with just a little more latex
the avatar would gather the confidence

to approach not flesh
but pixels or
whatever shows up
on an expensive screen
and it should be said
humans were not
ever acting as actors
on the other side
is there a third exit
anywhere including
stage bottom
For the entirety of an anchorless summer
the walls felt a rasp
as an ache formed

There Is A Problem Processing
Your Recent Payment

Writhing soothingly into the supposed goodness
                    of scent enrichment
            a destination wedding
                        takes place in the petri dish of my biopsy

All of the guests assimilate
            to being sprayed
with the gaseous contents of their choosing
            and probably
what I mean by this is if jumping into the leopard enclosure
            didn't guarantee their discontinuance
            into the leopard enclosure I'd go

I wish to be a meal for those with few meals

                    in part two
I begin to make associations between three to five facts

short selling our mutual downfall
            is a long held passion filled with renascences
and so I bring you a dead mouse
                    in the hopes you'll take me in forever
and scream *whatttuppSON*
                    when I disappear

                    Gallons of goings on afflict
volumes of *what if* statements to be spent on our rented carpet

                    We survive in remaining minds
        forfeiting the security deposit of a lifetime

Constant is the lack of

exit   shove that in your hole
                    for healthy participants of a trade war

                        Commit to Buddhism
            apparent is the deterioration but applaud for
I was locked in a room with five persons of seeming authority
                but managed to not once declare mutiny

                            and a pox on them all
                        as well as the building
                            cornered by the orbit
                        ordered to create a *Tinder*

                    No longer will I bow before
        six months of same-as-cash zero-APR-financing

Three organizational skills on which I could work include

                    do you ever feel as though your language
            is not the language of anyone you've ever met

Far As I Know There's Only One Widely Observed Holiday Focusing On A Zombie And On It There Is A Tendency Toward Brightness

Concrete Images
raided by ICE agents and
when otherwise sad humans
find no proper channel
no tube
down which to shove their mold
it's all internal of course
the intended meaning is   A Sin
no one is home
we are out
firebombing luxury views
managing the beet farm and
fucking being
productive components
of the circus wheel
My monkey   she's broken
watching *All In The Family*
while huffing that sweet dishrag
of power washed history
in the garage
a retired ICE agent
as played
by an ailing Denzel Washington
seeks redemption
But first
A set up

involving those who torched
the original trajectory
of our now failed adolescence
Sometimes
during certain scenes
of *All In The Family*
usually
when Mike
as played by Rob Reiner
is explaining to Archie
as played by Caroll O'Connor
what is or is not okay
like   you know
how nobody says *Fag* anymore or
whatever
during those scenes
ailing Denzel Washington
takes a pull
from a fifth of Jack and
fingers hotly his revolver
obviously he's thinking
of his daughter and
naturally she lives
on the opposite coast
so of course she's married
to a hedge fund manager and
only calls on Easter
retired ICE agent
ailing Denzel Washington suspects
his daughter resents his ass
even still
from when he used to hit mom
mom now has a place in Sonoma
with maybe too much natural light
she shares it with Bob

the organic frozen meal magnate
all of this is on repeat
in your brain and
will never recover the budget
Concrete Images
the futures as advertised
to our developing lobes
are all unattainable
                    like whoa
poppin' bottles
because the end

Vacay

When you begin to believe in the *Coeur De Lion*
the day is more likely a soaking napkin.

Everyone needs privacy
which is unfortunate
because everyone also needs to rub
up against someone else.

The latter is a fact
and I have done my best
to pretend otherwise.

I bought Bukowski's *Bone Palace Ballet*
at a Key West Books-A-Million,
a building I thought
strange to still be standing.

Haven't the people of Key West
set fire to this fucker yet?
I asked Sierra, stupid question, seeing
as we were standing inside.

This is an interlude
to tell you that some day
has got to be the worst day possible
and if you think that day's happened already
then it hasn't.

When situations get close to being considered the worst
they are more often simply Easter.

Sierra got scared.
There was an alligator sound
or she thought

there was an alligator sound.
Made us turn around.
Though I didn't know
how to turn around. I am bad
at reverse. I am bad
at skills. We were in the mangroves.
We were about a mile out
in the mangroves. It was reasonable
for there to be an alligator sound, it is not reasonable
to think the sun across my floor is a cat

when there's none.

Vanilla

These mornings
are the mornings Paul Manafort sees
whenever he's allowed
to log in
to *Credit Karma*

It's so true
that owl I'd bought
was part of a ruse
to get Hannah
to flog me bodiless

The reality of the reaction
was way more violent
than the fantasy of the dull and
I guess what's meant is

I have yet to apologize
for being so standard

No Soon Like Ø Too Soon

4 are dead and maybe more,
I don't know.
I haven't looked.
I'm afraid to look. Looking
makes it all knock
like an analogy
that won't leave us alone.
It happened to one of them
while plugging in
a brand new generator
purchased especially
for the occasion.
Here too, there's a generator
purchased especially
for occasions such as this
by the former owner
of these roofs, also dead
not from anything recent —
but from the natural ebb
of falling on 1's face
at 91. (He saw his wife
in the hospital
every day and possibly
that contributes.)
He should know
that we're safe now and
that having a generator
just makes us treat this
as though it were a party and
maybe it is. Funerals
can be parties too. I said to mom
a couple weeks ago
that I don't care none
for any final resting place

and just to please make sure —
if she were ever in a position
to plan my funeral —
that people could laugh
and people could talk shit,
and to make sure
to serve tacos and margs.
Back to the party:
I pre-gamed
by reading the daily email
from the Paris Review
'cause I can't afford
or don't actually want
a print subscription.
It was a poem
by Tim Dlugos and
Corragan was in the kitchen
frying eggs while
we could still fry eggs
and I quoted the poem,
said something
about queens and AIDS.
Inside of it, Tim said
something about AIDS
only being a fraction
of an unknown whole
but not that exactly
not so much
that I could get sued
by his estate
in the event he has one.
After that we shopped
for just the essentials
including a bag
of fiesta mix cheese,
cookies, a version
of Monopoly
catered toward kids,

wine and
were shut down
at self-checkout
by a woman
doing her god's work
'cause C. didn't have ID.
Walmart wasn't slangin'
this particular sin
but all the rest
for free is not at all
how whatever that song is
has ever gone before
in the history
of drunken appropriation.
In the comments section
of our local paper
there is a senior citizen
welled up behind the moat
of believing he's correct
all of the time and
I don't yet give up
but the prognosis
is increasingly
O NO A GHOST
inside the building.
Ghosts aside,
while actually
they're heeere:
for most of the day
I hung out
in a German-cut
dress. Others
went to work
pleasing others
by fixing electricity
not needed
for living. Tigers —
I imagine —

holed up
inside of holes.
Is this how 1 spells
going on without?
I looked or
I just tried to look
to make sure 4
is still correct
when it comes
to the # of dead and
I can't confirm
nor deny. The WiFi's
out. We're not. I feel
any day 1 don't drown
is okay regardless
if the ensemble
seems too formal.

Sunday Funday

                    On the first Gin & Juice
confusing the cats
by waking so early
'cause of some sea quest
about a father
who gets out of prison
and tortures his sons
with garden tools
insisting they show him
where the money's at
when, both in the quest
and in the life,
the money is nonexistent
and I think maybe
            I've been watching
                    too many Netflix originals.

The first thing I read today
was a line
from Yehuda Amichai
likening god's love
to an abusive relationship

then something surreal.

I don't look at the news
on weekends anymore
assuming someone who loves me
(not god) will at least text
in the event a nuclear winter
becomes our next season.

Anything else can wait
until Monday

when everything sux.
Outside these windows

my landlord's daughter plays
with some new gadget. I guess
they've just returned
from their Universalist Church.

In my head I applaud their faith
and with my hands

                   another Gin & Juice.

Yesterday Excitement
Couple's Boutique
backslash the only sex shop
in town was comparatively
poppin' off
by which I mean
I wasn't the only person in there
aside from the clerk
and I swelled with some sense
of solidarity. I may've been
the only one as drunk but still
I wasn't the only one
down for whatever
on a Saturday afternoon.

I eyed some of the lingerie
before realizing
I didn't know my size.

I stumbled over a shelf
next to the bathroom

no, wait...

that happened in the bookstore
where I walked out

with Robbe-Grillet's *The Voyeur*
and in the same way
people tend to buy
what appears to be a meal
in the making
when only in the grocery store
for cat toys,
condoms, and wine. Also
I made sure to get a copy
of Chomsky's *Understanding Power*
so as not to freak out
the clerk who, really,
doesn't give a damn
what I buy from her store
so long as I just
get

out.

But back to Excitement:

I declined
all of the lingerie
'cause most of it
was out of my price range and
since I don't know my size,
though I really should by now,
I didn't ask
but doubt the place
takes returns.

Most of my friends are married.
Half own homes.
Three quarters have children.
One quarter is composed of lawyers,
another — doctors. The rest

are something grand.

Namely I've been on the decline.
Blake now lives an hour away
and is grateful she met Rob on the train
and is growing her own tea
and owns a loom
and drives a '69 Beetle
with a trans radio sitting in the backseat

while yesterday I considered Yoga Nidra
but instead went to Excitement Couple's Boutique
stag and disgusted with myself

buying some toy
I can't afford
endorsed by that one woman

always on the TV
always stoked
always endorsing
a former sniper

As I use the toy I think I feel
unlike how my landlord's daughter might feel.

Now I'm back
reading *Blackwater*
throwing a third Gin & Juice

onto the faces
                of Erik Prince.

Is BDSM A Privilege Of The
Emotionally Well To Do
Or,
How Much Did This Dining Set
Cost To Rent

When you went to work
I reached for our new anal plug
in search of some threshold
to which the National Guard
had not yet been deployed

Should we be concerned
if free radicals spread
into the Dead Sea

In case of emergency
set fire to the compendium

I remember reading
about how Kathy would compose
with a vibrator in her person
and this is hardly that
not all the turds can glow

What hasn't been Pompei'd
is scheduled to be Pompei'd
while the population hibernates
sycophants administer our water
tryn'a poison our safe-hole

Katy'd always say *so what*
Whenever I'd preach Kathy's practice

I'd been so occupied with becoming feral
I'd failed her in tandem
I'd failed to shout *Dolla bill y'all*

The basin of insertion needs dowsing
while you're out in the world
bringing pain therapy to the willing
I'm ducking into the cocoon
getting depraved with my sallow self

Name Checking The Void

Whoo-oo-oo-oo-hooh-hoo-oo! Oh, look at me, I am perishing in this gateway. — Mikhail Bulgakov

There is a murder
on The Orient Express
taking place in my apartment
and I've forgotten
everything anyone
else might consider
a form of accomplishment
so now *You Are Here*

vomiting veggie fajitas
into the nearest hole
and wanting, wanting,
wanting so much
but not knowing
how to walk out of a door.

Agoraphobic tendencies
replace job interviews
while according
to *Forbes.com*
my landscape is one
composed of burnt bridges.
There is comfort
in knowing Rory
also sleeps with Wookiees
and nobody's immune
regardless
of what they're sittin' on
in the bank.

I would like to apologize
to my left arm
for the damage done
while Emily
and Lorelei have it out
over behavior
while memorializing
a lion. Speaking

of memorializing
big game, I'm loath
to admit I didn't hear
about the owner
of *Jimmy John's*
and his canned hunts
until last Saturday.
I've consumed
so many *unwhichs*
over the years —
veggie or not —
I am so complicit. Thankfully
I've been fired
through fault
of my own and
that of a careless dealer.
No more temptation
and if I find out
the owner of *SoPies*
uses profits
from my pizza orders
to murder
endangered species
then record it
while giving a thumbs up
like the guys
from *Reel Big Fish* did
in '96, then
I'll have to leave the house
in search of sustenance.

Comedy is no longer an option
while I await the news

that even this vegetable garden
is guilty of sexual assault.

I am frightened of distance
divided by your echo chamber.

Information
re: the world
gets itself ingested
by the ocelot
of my loins
dragging the possum
of my conscience
through a 2X2.

What's capitalized
in the currents
of capitalism
is no longer
as Janis says
of great social
and political import

meanwhile I balk
at stepping into the sun:

intangible goals and ass
subtracted from itching days.

Surfacing allegations
impel my surrender
to your absence
which is constant
and screaming.

Whatever, I guess
all interlopers
sleeping on the lawn
can stay.

I'll build a tent city
inside of which
we can yell
into cups
and out of our family.

Yesterday, finally
I finished *Anne Sexton:*
A Self-Portrait In Letters
and though I haven't seen it
I imagine

the experience was similar
to buying popcorn
before walking in
to opening night
of Mel Gibson's *The Passion*
Of The Christ.

Censorship does disgust
but still
I wish someone would cut
five to six minutes
worth of violence
from the everyday.

Luke protests fabrication
of a new human life
while Paris pushes
DVDs of *Gone Girl*

as I eye-salt the cider

sip, sip, and melt. Eye-salt
added to all liquids,

multiplied by the hope
for which Rory makes way

as we choose decline.

The Day I Killed A Tiger

Choose a hole. Disintegrate.
Repeat. This is how
I begin descent into you.

I desire humor
but being's otherwise.

Even bowling's a dung strong sierra.

20-somethings dominate the crowd.

As that disco ball swings low
this sweet chariot comes with free shipping
if you order your penance now.

It was in Hanoi that we woke
from jaded being cool
to a movement so fire
we were too embarrassed
to fail to mourn. What this means
is that my wake will serve tacos
and this year's award
for fastest encroaching conglomerate
goes to the murder
with which your cousin gets away.
An EEO complaint was filed inside a ditch
while passed ass out on a wicker chair
and being eaten alive
by living things.

Through a can of *Natty Light*
your cousin confessed
into your bitten face
before speeding off
with our stolen merch.

This is the territory
in which we divide
and refuse to conquer.

Blood hot with coupons
I set fire to the lake behind the lake
on top of the farm
inside of the brain.

The day I killed a tiger

we went to Red Bowl
where I'd had enough
of death and said

*How about
these fucking lights?*

*From now on
let's get our Mei Fun to go.*

Heart attacks abound
and everyone was kind. Everyone
was handing out hugs.

Apples with horsemeat
were the nightly special
and the pelt was cut perfect.

Perfunctory masturbation
took place in the homeland

and I became one
with the last of two eggs.

Funds were raised.
Golden arches got erected.
Someone OD'd.

Tuxes rented, not returned.
Hairs curled.
Fluids dripped simply.

Visibility aches. For years
I was blind. This year
I'm blind.

Acknowledgements

Some of these poems originally showed up in *The Fanzine*,
WUSSY Mag, *Cordite Poetry Review*, *Wag's Revue*,
The A3 Review, *mutiny!* and *Twyckenham Notes*